Creative Crafts for Kids

Spooky CRAFTS

By Helen Skillicorn

Gareth Stevens
Publishing

Please visit our Web site www.garethstevens.com. For a free color catalog of all our high-quality books, call toll free 1-800-542-2595 or fax 1-877-542-2596.

Library of Congress Cataloging-in-Publication Data
Skillicorn, Helen.
    Spooky crafts / Helen Skillicorn.
        p. cm. — (Creative crafts for kids)
    Includes index.
    ISBN 978-1-4339-3564-0 (library binding) -- ISBN 978-1-4339-3565-7 (pbk.) --
    ISBN 978-1-4339-3566-4 (6-pack)
    1. Halloween decorations—Juvenile literature. 2. Halloween costumes—Juvenile literature. 3. Handicraft—Juvenile literature. I. Title.
    TT900.H32S55 2010
    745.594'1646—dc22
                                                                                        2009039233

J
745.5941
SKI

Published in 2010 by
Gareth Stevens Publishing
111 East 14th Street, Suite 349
New York, NY 10003

© 2010 The Brown Reference Group Ltd.

For Gareth Stevens Publishing:
Art Direction: Haley Harasymiw
Editorial Direction: Kerri O'Donnell

For The Brown Reference Group Ltd:
Editorial Director: Lindsey Lowe
Managing Editor: Tim Harris
Children's Publisher: Anne O'Daly
Design Manager: David Poole
Production Director: Alastair Gourlay

Picture Credits:
All photographs: Martin Norris
Front Cover: Shutterstock: Kudryashka and Martin Norris

Manufactured in the United States of America
1 2 3 4 5 6 7 8 9 12 11 10

CPSIA compliance information: Batch #BRW0102GS: For further information contact Gareth Stevens, New York, New York at 1-800-542-2595.

Contents

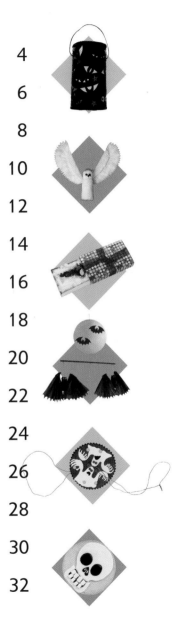

Introduction

This Spooky Crafts book is packed full of projects to send a shiver up your spine on a spooky night! Try making a Ghostly whirrer that makes the sound of a ghost swooshing past, or an Owl puppet with flapping wings, and even a crunchy Bonehead cookie! For Halloween, there are dressing-up ideas and tricks to give your family and friends a fright.

YOU WILL NEED

Each project includes a list of all the things you need.

Before you buy new materials, look around your home to see what you could use instead. For example, you can cut cardboard shapes out of an empty cereal carton.

You can buy craft foam at a craft shop and other items, such as felt and fake fur fabric, at a department store. For the Count costume, we have used black lining fabric to make the cloak. You can buy lining fabric from a department store, too.

Getting started

 Read the steps for the project first.

 Gather together all the items you need.

 Cover your work surface with newspaper.

 Wear an apron, or change into old clothes.

A message for adults

All the projects in Spooky Crafts have been designed for children to make, but occasionally they will need you to help. Some of the projects do require the use of sharp utensils, such as scissors or needles. Please read through the instructions before your child starts work.

Making patterns

Follow these steps to make the patterns on pages 30 and 31. Using a pencil, trace the pattern onto tracing paper. If you're making a project out of fabric, you can cut out the tracing paper pattern and pin it onto the fabric. To cut the pattern out of cardboard, turn the tracing over, and lay it onto the cardboard. Rub firmly over the pattern with a pencil. The shape will appear on the cardboard. Cut out the shape.

When you have finished

Wash paintbrushes, and put everything away.

Put pens, pencils, paints, and glue in an old box or ice-cream container.

Keep scissors and any other sharp items in a safe place.

Stick needles and pins into a pincushion or a piece of scrap cloth.

BE SAFE

Look out for the safety boxes. They will appear whenever you need to ask an adult for help.

Ask an adult to help you use sharp scissors.

Creepy claws

These could be monster hands or witchy claws with long, curly nails. You can make them from craft foam, and they're perfect for dressing up for Halloween.

YOU WILL NEED

green and purple craft foam	scissors
	felt-tip pen
Velcro	clear glue
hole punch	masking tape

1 First draw around both your hands onto green craft foam. If you are right-handed, drawing around your right hand will be tricky, so ask a friend to help you. Cut out the foam hands.

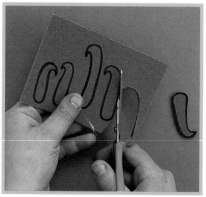

2 Draw ten curly fingernails onto purple craft foam, and cut them out. Glue them onto the tips of the fingers and thumbs. Let the glue dry.

3 To make warts for the witchy hands, cut out small, roundish pieces of green and purple foam. Use a hole punch to cut out very tiny circles of foam. Glue the circles onto the hands, a small piece on top of a bigger piece.

4 Cut out a thin strip of green craft foam long enough to fit around your finger. Glue the strip to the back of a witchy finger to make a ring. Stick the ring in place with masking tape while the glue dries to keep it from popping off. Make a ring for each finger and thumb. Take off the masking tape when the glue has dried.

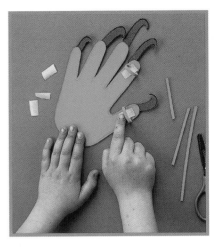

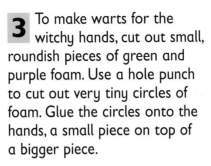

5 To make wrist straps, cut eight strips of green craft foam. Stick a piece of Velcro to the end of each strip. Glue two pieces with hooked Velcro to one side of a witchy hand with the Velcro pointing upward. Glue two pieces with loopy Velcro to the other side of the hand with the Velcro pointing down. Do the same on the other hand. Put in your hand, and fasten the wrist straps.

7

Flashlight lantern

When you're out on a dark night, carry this glittery lantern with its glowing, spooky eyes.

YOU WILL NEED

- big plastic soda bottle
- scissors
- kitchen foil
- thin black cardboard
- silver spray paint
- glue
- colored cellophane
- shoelace or cord
- black glitter and sequins
- small flashlight
- toothpick

1 Cut off the bottom half of a large plastic bottle—make sure this piece is taller than your flashlight. Put a piece of kitchen foil in the bottom of the bottle to reflect the light.

2 Cut out a piece of black cardboard long enough to go around the bottle and about ⅓in (1cm) taller. Spray one side with silver spray paint. It is best to do this outside. The silver side will be the inner wall of the lantern and will reflect the light. Draw on pairs of spooky eyes, and cut them out.

8

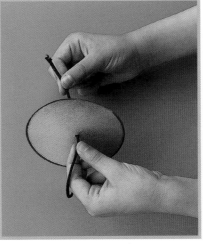

3 Glue pieces of colored cellophane or candy wrappers over the cut-out eyes.

4 To make a lid, draw around the end of the bottle onto black cardboard. Cut out the circle, and spray one side silver. Make a hole in the center using a toothpick, and push a piece of shoelace or cord through. Tie a knot under the lid.

5 Glue the cardboard cover around the bottle—it will be slightly taller than the bottle at the top. To decorate, dab on glue and sprinkle on black glitter. You can glue on sequins, too.

Ask an adult to make two holes for the handle.

6 Place the flashlight upright in the lantern. Scrunch up see-through cellophane, and push it around the handle of the flashlight so that it stands up. Glue a shoelace around the inside of the cardboard at the top to make a rim for the lid. Ask an adult to make two holes in the plastic sides of the lantern. Thread a shoelace through to make a carrying handle.

9

Count costume

Slick back your hair, and find some dark trousers to go with this Count Dracula costume. It's perfect for a spooky Halloween party.

YOU WILL NEED

3ft x 6ft (1m x 2m) light black fabric

fabric glue

white and black felt

red craft foam

tracing paper

pencil

scrap white paper

scissors

white ribbon

black ribbon

pins and a needle

white and black thread

pinking shears

1 Trace the shirt front and collar patterns on page 30. Transfer the tracings onto paper. Cut them out. Place the paper templates along the fold of a piece of white felt. Draw around the templates, and cut out the felt shapes. Make a snip in the fold in the collar, and fold back the corners to make pointy collar tips. Pin the collar to the neck of the shirt front—the free ends of the collar will go around your neck. Ask an adult to help you sew the collar to the neck edge of the shirt front. Take out the pins as you go.

2 Sew two pieces of white ribbon to the ends of the collar so you can tie the shirt front around your neck. Trace the

pattern for the bat bow tie on page 30, and cut it out of black felt. Cut out three circles of black felt to make shirt buttons. Glue the bow tie and buttons onto the shirt front.

Ask an adult to help you with the sewing.

3 To make the cloak collar, cut a rectangle of red craft foam 12in x 4in (30cm x 10cm). Cut the two bottom corners off so that the collar is wider at the top. Glue the foam collar onto black felt. Let the glue dry, and then cut out the felt around the foam, leaving 1in (2.5cm) extra felt at the bottom.

HANDY HINT

Ask an adult to iron back the pointy collar tips to make firm folds.

4 To make the cloak, run a needle and thread in a big running stitch along one long edge of the black fabric. Tie a knot in the thread at one end, then pull on the other end so that the material bunches up. When the bunched material is about as wide as the short edge of the red collar, tie a knot in the thread to keep the material in place.

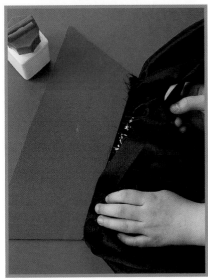

5 Glue the bunched fabric onto the bottom of the red collar. Glue a long piece of black ribbon on top of the bunched fabric to clamp the cloak to the collar. The ribbon will tie around your neck.

6 Trim the edges of the cloak with pinking shears to make a zigzag edge. We have cut big, curved scallops along the bottom edge of the cloak like a bat's wings.

Owl puppet

This ghostly white owl spreads its wings and swivels its head. Dress up in black on a dark night to work the puppet—it will look as if the owl is swooping by itself!

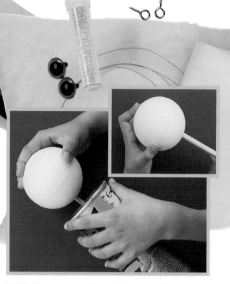

1 First, cut 2in (5cm) off the bottom of the chip container. The rest of the tube will be the owl's body. Push the short dowel rod into the polystyrene ball. The ball is the owl's head. Fit the head into the body as shown.

2 Push a white sock over the owl's head and part of its body. Leave the sock quite loose so that you can swivel the owl's head by turning the dowel rod.

YOU WILL NEED

tube chip container	fabric glue	two toy eyes
dowel rod 8in (20cm) long	white fake fur and felt	felt-tip pen
2 dowel rods 30in (76cm) long	white feathers	modeling clay and black paint
2 screw eyes	scissors and pencil	wire
white toweling sock	tracing paper	needle and thread
polystyrene ball	tape and pins	
	scrap white paper	

4 Trace the wing patterns on pages 30 and 31. Cut out the shapes, and tape them together to make one template for the outer wing and one for the inner wing. Pin the outer wing template to white felt, and cut around it. Cut out a second outer wing. The inner wing is a half pattern, so fold a piece of white fake fur, and pin on the template with the straight edge against the fold. Cut around the template. Cut out two. Paste fabric glue along the curved edge of the felt outer wing. Lay it on top of the inner wing, fold the inner wing over, and press down. Make up the second wing in the same way.

3 Cut a piece of white fake fur to cover the body. Paste the underside of the fabric with glue, and wrap it around the chip container. Cut out a rectangle of fur fabric to cover the head, and cut out a figure-eight shape for the eyes. Glue the fabric over the top of the head. Glue down the sides—the corners of the fabric make two pointy ears.

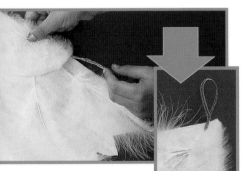

5 To decorate the wings, glue on white feathers. Thread wire through the fold in the fur to give a stiff edge. At the thin end of each wing, bend the wire into a loop (see inset picture). Ask an adult to trim it. At the wide end of the wing, bend the wire into a hook.

6 Sew the loops of wire to the back of the owl (near the top of the body) with strong thread. To make rods to work the puppet, push a screw eye into the end of a long dowel rod, and screw it in place. Make two. Hook each wing onto a rod.

7 Glue eyes onto the owl's face, and glue on a piece of feather between the eyes. Shape a beak out of modeling clay. Let the clay beak dry and harden, and paint it black. Glue it on.

Mystery box

You can make your ghost stories extra scary by telling your friends to feel inside the mystery box. Pretend that a creature or some ghostly slime from the story is lurking in the box! Try out a bowl of jello or baked beans inside for gruesome effects.

YOU WILL NEED

cardboard box
crêpe paper
scissors
masking tape
plastic bag

white sticky-backed plastic
felt-tip pen
ruler

1 Rule a line around the cardboard box 1in (2.5cm) from the top. Cut off the top of the box—it will be the lid of the mystery box.

2 Tape down the flaps at the bottom of the box and the flaps in the lid. Draw a circle in the center of the lid big enough for your hand. You can do this by drawing around a mug. Cut out the circle.

14

3 Cover the box and lid with blue crêpe paper. Push your scissors through the crêpe paper over the hole in the lid. Snip to the edge and then tape back the crêpe fringe inside the lid.

4 Cut an elbow's length of plastic bag. Stick small tabs of masking tape along one edge of the plastic, and stick it inside the lid around the hole to make a tube for your arm. Line the inside of the bottom of the box with plastic, too, to protect it from the gooey things you're going to put inside.

5 Draw big ghosts and pairs of spooky eyes onto white sticky-backed plastic. Cut out the shapes, peel off the backing, and stick them around the outside of the box.

6 Add extra decoration with a gold pen or some gold paint. We have written "One ghostly night" on our box to begin a scary ghost story.

Trick finger

"Trick or treat?" This gory finger in a gift box is a fantastic trick for Halloween. Hold the pretty present underneath so you can poke your index finger up through the hole in the base.

YOU WILL NEED

cotton wool	scissors
fake blood	paper glue
gift wrapping paper	felt-tip pen
large, empty matchbox	poster paints
	paintbrush
ribbon	

1 Cut out a fingerwide section in the matchbox cover. The section should stretch about three-quarters the length of the cover.

2 Slip the cover onto the matchbox with the cut-out slit on the bottom. Draw a circle onto the base of the matchbox at one end of the slit. Cut out the circle to make a hole.

16

3 Paint the matchbox base white on the outside and red on the inside.

4 Spread glue onto the matchbox cover, and wrap it with gift wrapping paper. To add a ribbon, tie two pieces of ribbon together to make a cross that goes on top of the matchbox, and glue the ends underneath the matchbox.

5 Fill the matchbox with cotton wool, and poke a hole through the cotton wool over the hole in the base of the matchbox. Drip fake blood onto the cotton wool around the hole so it looks as if your finger has been cut off!

Witch piñata

A piñata is a paper toy filled with candies, and this one is for a Halloween party. To play, each of you takes a swing at the piñata—it's even more fun if you wear a blindfold. When the piñata breaks, everyone rushes to gather up the goodies.

YOU WILL NEED

newspaper	scissors
PVA glue	bowl
paintbrush	masking tape
poster paints	tissue paper
balloon	string
witch's hat	darning needle
purple crêpe paper	

1 To make the witch's head from papier-mâché, first tape a balloon into a bowl to keep it steady. Tear newspaper into strips, and mix up half water and half PVA glue. Paste the paper strips all over the balloon, leaving only a circle at the base uncovered. Paste on four layers of papier-mâché. Let it dry overnight, and then pop the balloon.

18

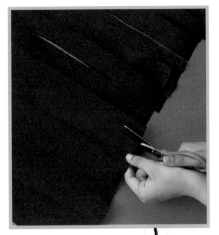

2 The gap in the papier-mâché ball is the top of the witch's head. To make the witch's features, dip tissue paper in the paste, scrunch it up, and shape it to make a nose, eyes, and mouth. Press the features onto the paper ball. Let them dry.

3 Paint the witch's face green using poster paints. Paint on features in different colors, too.

4 To make witchy hair, cut strips running most of the way up a large sheet of purple crêpe paper.

6 Now fill up the piñata with candies and perhaps a few small toys. To hang up the piñata, make a hole on either side of the witch's head using a darning needle. Make a hole on either side of the brim of the witch's hat, too. Thread string through the brim, then through the piñata, and then through the brim on the other side. Tie the ends of string together, and hang up the piñata.

5 Stick pieces of masking tape along the uncut edge of the crêpe paper, and tape it inside the head at the top.

Make sure everyone stands clear of the swinging stick.

19

Bat mobile

Make a mobile of bats flitting around a big full moon. It will look fabulous and ghostly hanging in your bedroom.

YOU WILL NEED

black fake fur	dowel rod painted black
black pipe cleaners	black thread
silver cardboard	white cardboard
black paper	paintbrush
scissors	glow-in-the-dark paint
four pieces of black tissue paper 8in x 15in (20cm x 38cm)	pencil
	PVA glue
needle	metal ring from a keyring

1 To make a furry bat, roll up a small piece of black fake fur fabric. Sew it to keep the fabric rolled up. Make two bats.

2 Bend a black pipe cleaner, and sew it to the bat's body. You will hang the bat's wings from the pipe cleaner arms. Do the same to the second bat. Dab a little PVA glue onto the bat's furry head, and pinch the fur to make pointy ears.

3 To make a wing, fold a piece of black tissue paper into a concertina shape. To do this, start by folding one long side over about 1in (2.5cm), then turn over the tissue paper, and fold the edge again. Keep turning and folding until you have a single strip. Make four wings.

4 Cut a curve at one thin end of each strip. This will give the bats pointy wing tips. Glue one end of a wing along a pipe cleaner arm. The wing will fan out as in the picture. You can glue tiny cardboard eyes onto the bats, too. We have painted our bat's eyes with glow-in-the-dark paint.

5 Cut a large circle from silver cardboard to make the moon. You can do this by drawing around a dinner plate. Cut out four bats from black paper, and glue them onto both sides of the moon.

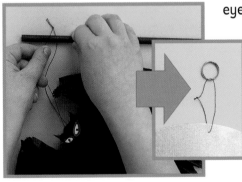

6 Sew thread to each bat, and tie the threads to the ends of the dowel. Ask an adult to cut notches in the dowel to keep the bats in place. Sew thread into the moon at the top and bottom. Tie the thread at the bottom to the middle of the dowel, and tie the thread at the top to a metal ring so you can hang up the mobile.

21

Monster mask

Make this ridiculous monster face with its goggly eyes and flapping ears. Our mask is made from craft foam, so it's very light and comfortable to wear.

YOU WILL NEED

blue, red, white, and green craft foam	black marker pen
	black cardboard
scissors and pencil	white muslin
glue	hole puncher
	blue ribbon

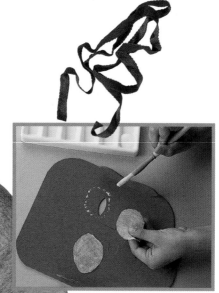

1 Draw the shape of the mask onto blue craft foam. Make sure it is big enough to cover your face. Cut it out. Draw on two eyes, a nose, and a slit for the mouth—hold the mask up to your face to make sure that the features are in the right place. Cut out the eyes and mouth. Cut around the nose except at the top so you make a nose flap. Draw two ears at the edge of the foam. Cut them out.

2 Glue the ears onto the mask by their straight edges, ½in (1cm) from the sides. When the mask is bent around your face, the ears will stick out. Cut out two wobbly circles of muslin bigger than the eye holes. Glue them over the eyes—one higher than the other.

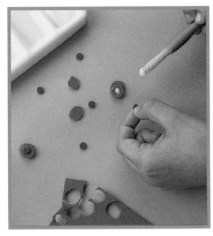

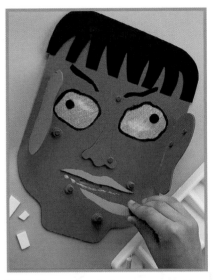

3 To make monster pimples, cut out little circles of blue and red foam. Glue them to the mask in little piles, with smaller circles on top. To make circles of red foam, use a hole puncher.

4 Cut a hair piece out of black cardboard. To get the shape of the head right, draw around the top of the mask.

5 Go around the edge of the eyes with a marker pen, and draw on goggly pupils. Draw on eyebrows, too. Cut out lips, teeth, and a scar from colored foam. Glue them onto the mask. Glue the two lips above and below the mouth slit.

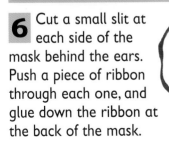

6 Cut a small slit at each side of the mask behind the ears. Push a piece of ribbon through each one, and glue down the ribbon at the back of the mask.

23

Ghostly whirrer

To work the whirrer, hold a loop of thread in each hand. Twist the circle of cardboard at least 20 times so that the thread winds up. Pull the strings, and watch the whirrer spin. Listen for a spooky sound, too.

YOU WILL NEED

thin purple cardboard	purple craft foam
white paper	24in (60cm) string
felt-tip pen	
pinking shears	glue
scissors	paintbrush
hole puncher	sequins
needle	

1 Draw around a mug or lid onto purple cardboard. Do this twice to make two circles.

2 Cut out the two circles using pinking shears. Glue them together. If you don't have pinking shears, cut out the circles using scissors. Glue the two circles together, and then cut a zigzag edge.

3 Cut out four small ghosts from white paper, and glue two on each side of the whirrer. Glue on sequins for ghostly eyes.

4 Use a hole puncher to make holes around the edge of the circle. Now use the puncher to cut out four small circles of purple craft foam.

5 Glue the purple foam dots to the center of the circle, about 1in (2.5cm) apart. Glue the other two foam dots to the other side in the same place. Thread the string onto a needle, and push the needle through one foam dot and out the other side and then back through the other dot. Tie the two ends of string together, leaving a loop on either side of the disk.

Flaming cauldron

This is a wonderful project for Halloween. When you're collecting treats, put them all in this bubbling, boiling cauldron.

YOU WILL NEED

plastic bowl	purple cardboard
three corks	red cellophane
masking tape	PVA glue
clear glue	paintbrush
silver spray paint	muslin fabric
felt-tip pen	black poster paint
coat hanger	

1 Glue three corks to the base of a plastic bowl to make legs for the cauldron. Keep the corks in place with masking tape while the glue dries.

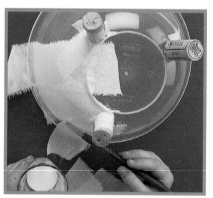

2 Mix two parts PVA glue with one part water to make a paste. Tear muslin into strips. Paste the strips over the outside of the bowl and legs. One layer of fabric is enough.

3 When the muslin has dried, paint the outside of the cauldron black, then spray it silver. Remember to lay down newspaper and keep the windows open. You may find it easier to spray paint ouside.

4 Draw bats onto colored cardboard, and cut them out. Glue the bats onto the cauldron.

Ask an adult to help you make the handle.

5 Scrunch up red cellophane, and glue it to the base of the cauldron to make flames. Ask an adult to cut a piece of coat hanger to make a handle and to make two holes in the side of the bowl. Bend the coat hanger wire into a curve with the two ends pointing in. They fit into the holes in the side of the bowl.

27

Bonehead cookie

Munch and crunch through a scary skull. You can use this decoration idea on top of a plain sponge cake or on a big store-bought cookie.

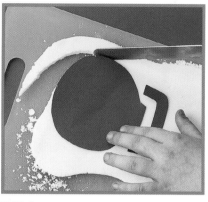

1 Sprinkle icing sugar on a kitchen surface and onto your rolling pin. Roll out the white cake fondant. Draw a skull onto colored paper. Draw the head and a separate jaw shape. Cut them out, and lay them onto the fondant. Cut around the shapes with a knife.

YOU WILL NEED

scissors and pencil	white cake fondant
colored paper	black food coloring
spreading knife	
rolling pin	basting brush
icing sugar	mixing bowl
big cookie or cake	teaspoon
marshmallows	black writing icing

2 Dip the brush in water, and paste the icing pieces. Press them onto the cookie.

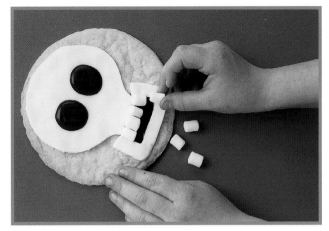

3 Mix up some icing using icing sugar and a little water. Add a couple of drops of black food coloring to make the icing black. Drizzle the black icing onto the skull to make two eye sockets and a mouth.

4 Press small white marshmallows onto the wet black icing to make teeth.

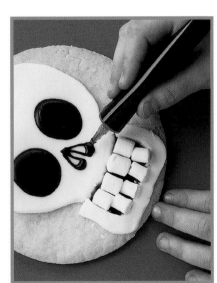

5 Draw a nose cavity onto the skull using black writing icing, or you can use the black icing you have made, and drizzle it on carefully.

Patterns

Here are the patterns you will need to make some of the projects. To find out how to make a pattern, follow the instructions in the "Making patterns" box on page 5. Some of the patterns are half patterns. There are instructions to help you use the half patterns in the steps for the projects.

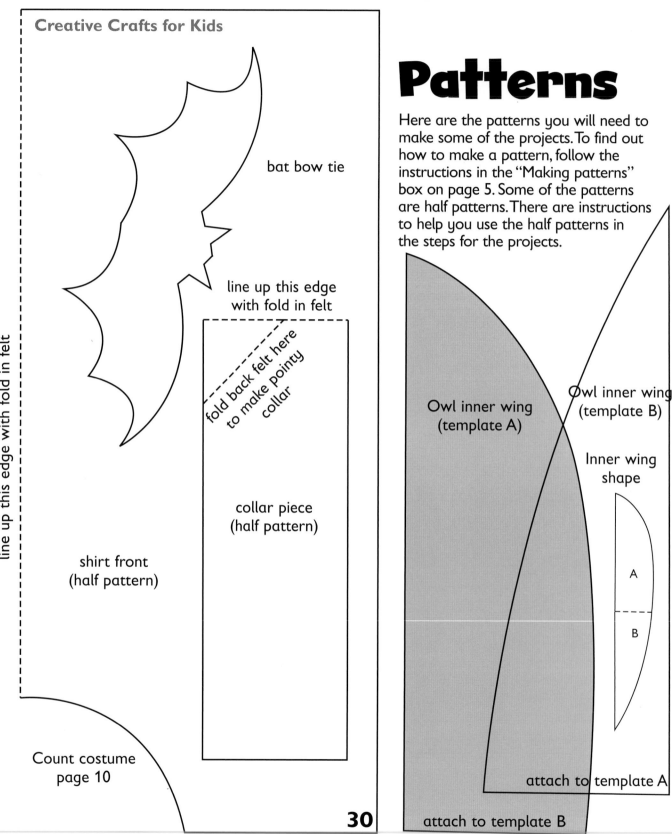

bat bow tie

line up this edge with fold in felt

line up this edge with fold in felt

fold back felt here to make pointy collar

collar piece (half pattern)

shirt front (half pattern)

Count costume page 10

Owl inner wing (template A)

Owl inner wing (template B)

Inner wing shape

A

B

attach to template A

attach to template B

30

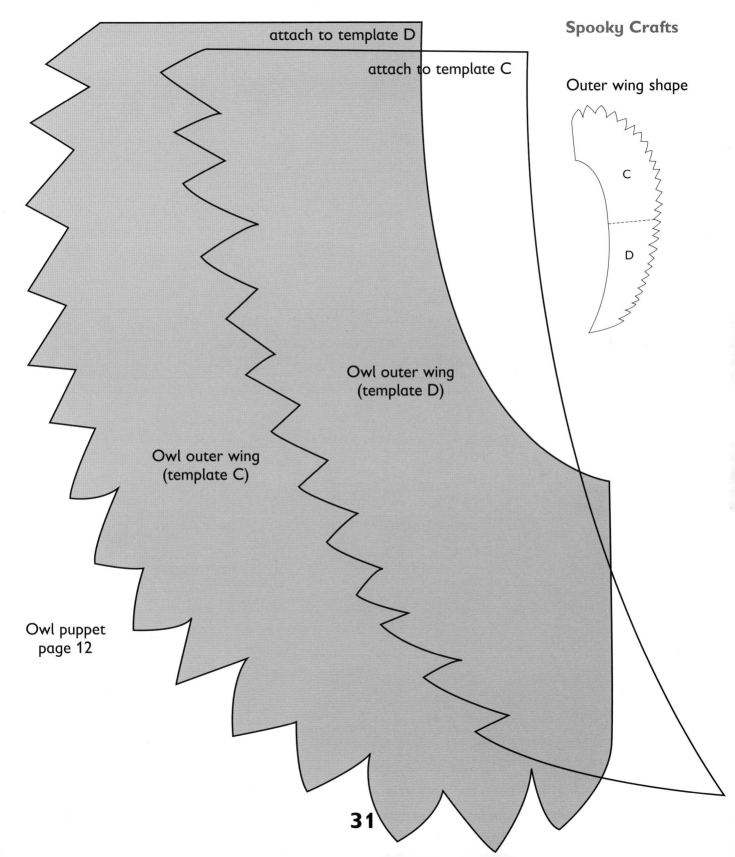

attach to template D

attach to template C

Outer wing shape

C

D

Owl outer wing
(template D)

Owl outer wing
(template C)

Owl puppet
page 12

31

Glossary

cauldron a large metal pot in which liquids are boiled

cellophane a thin, transparent, waterproof material used for wrapping and covering

fondant a smooth paste made from syrup used as a coating for cakes, nuts, or fruit

fringe a decorative border consisting of short strands of thread or other material

gory covered in blood

gruesome frightening or shocking

muslin a thin, plain-weave cotton cloth used for curtains, sheets, and dresses

papier-mâché sheets of paper pulp and glue stuck together in layers, usually onto a mold, to make objects

piñata a decorated container of sweets or gifts that is hit and broken with sticks

pinking shears scissors with blades that cut zigzag edges in cloth

polystyrene a manufactured material, often in the form of rigid white foam

PVA glue one of the most common glues. "PVA" stands for polyvinyl acetate.

scallop a decorative wavy edge in a fabric

Velcro a material of two strips, one consisting of hooks and the other consisting of loops, that fasten together

Index